Discover Life

A Study
of the
Ten Commandments

J. Laurence Martin, Editor

HERALD PRESS
Scottdale, Pennsylvania
Kitchener, Ontario

Photographs: cover by Hans Rathgeb; page 32, courtesy of United Artists; page 66, H. Armstrong Roberts. The questionnaires on pages 12, 36, and 42 are used by permission from **Rap**, a mini-course in Christian lifestyle, by Lyman Coleman.

Except as otherwise noted, the Scripture quotations in this book are from **The New English Bible**, used by permission. © The Delegates of the Oxford University Press and the Syndics of the Cambridge University Press, 1961, 1970.

The outline for this book is based on "International Sunday School Lessons; the International Bible Lessons for Christian Teaching," copyright 1967 by the Committee on the Uniform Series. Used by permission.

CONTENTS

Discovery Phases

Every lesson has three phases of development. Each phase is important to study.

**Phase One:
Personal
Discovery**

Each lesson has some key Bible passages for your personal study. This phase is meant to be done during the week as preparation for the lesson to be discussed. Look for the Phase One symbol in each lesson.

**Phase Two:
Discover Through
Study and
Discussion**

The lessons attempt to unlock the meaning of the Ten Commandments, the teachings of Jesus, and related New Testament instructions for you. The first part of the class period can be used for questioning and discussing the issues raised by the writers. Look for the Phase Two symbol in each lesson.

**Phase Three:
Discovery Groups**

Do you feel the need for the fellowship and the support of a small group? Why not form discovery groups consisting of at least four persons? These persons should remain as a group for at least four sessions. Some may wish to be together for the entire study. Your group must decide. If your class is too small to form several groups, consider the total class as a discovery group. Suggestions will be in each lesson to help your discovery group become a helping community.

As members you can share your personal discoveries made in Phase One. The knowledge and insights of Phase Two can help in enlarging your concepts and world view. Phase Three is where you can help each other discover the practical ways to live life in God's will, as you share your successes, failures, and questions with fellow members of your discovery group. Look for ways to be helpful to members of your group throughout the week. Look for the Phase Three symbol in each lesson.

1. Why Have Laws?

By Glen R. Horst

Exodus 20:1, 2

God spoke, and these were his words:

I am the Lord your God who brought you out of Egypt, out of the land of slavery.

Deuteronomy 5:32 -- 6:3

You shall be careful to do as the Lord your God has commanded you; do not turn from it to right or to left. You must conform to all the Lord your God commands you, if you would live and prosper and remain long in the land you are to occupy.

These are the commandments, statutes, and laws which the Lord your God commanded me to teach you to observe in the land into which you are passing to occupy it, a land flowing with milk and honey, so that you may fear the Lord your God and keep all his statutes and commandments which I am giving you, both you, your sons, and your descendants all your lives, and so that you may live long. If you listen, O Israel, and are careful to observe them, you will prosper and increase greatly as the Lord the God of your fathers promised you.

Matthew 5:17

"Do not suppose that I have come to abolish the Law and the prophets; I did not come to abolish, but to complete."

PHASE 1

Read Exodus 19 -- 20:2 carefully.

1. What did God do for the Hebrew slaves in Egypt?

2. What did God want the Hebrew slaves to become? _____

_____

3. You are a member of the crowd assembled at the foot of Mount Sinai worshiping God. What feelings do you have?

fear _____, reverence _____, excitement _____, other feelings _____

Hearing God's Word

4. If you were a Hebrew slave having experienced God's help in becoming free, how would you respond to the Ten Commandments?

_____ Resentment

_____ Obey unwillingly

_____ Unconcerned about them

_____ Obey joyfully

_____ Question God's right to make laws.

Read Psalm 19:7-14 to discover the value of the law.

1. The psalmist loves the law for the following reasons:

_____

_____

2. My attitude toward the law of God is:

_____

_____

_____

Pray and Reflect

What personal attitudes have you discovered that you have toward laws in general? Toward the Ten Commandments?

Doing God's Word

Do you feel changes in your attitudes are necessary? If so, what are they?

We live in an age when policemen are called "pigs" and when many lawyers are known as shysters. Vandalism, juvenile delinquency, and civil disobedience plague many communities. Citizens call for "law and order," but rationalize their way around the income tax laws and glance in their mirrors as they break the traffic laws. Politicians ignore treaties with North American natives and openly violate international laws. Modern man's view of law has become a rather cynical one. Law is seen as an impersonal force designed to crush our freedom and initiative.

Are Laws for Real?

Authority is "the big stick," to break unless we happen to be wielding it. Youth are said to have a larger dose of this authority hang-up than other people. Maybe that's true -- after all, the teen years are the time to try your wings and to cut the apron strings. Doing these things looks like an authority hang-up (especially to adults). Yet, adults have their authority hang-ups too. What about the way labor and management get along in the work situation? What about adult reactions to government policies which affect their freedom? What about the way Mom and Dad decide who "wears the pants"?

Authority Hang-Up

Authority hang-ups creep into our church-life too. The predominant style of church-life has often tended to be authoritarian. It has thrived on "do's" and "don'ts" (mostly on the "don'ts"). However, authoritarian Christianity has often become sapless and joyless. Christians are refusing to picture God as the authoritarian mother who said: "Find out what the baby's doing and make him stop." With this kind of reaction to law and authority, how do we feel when we discover that the lessons in this book "zero in" on the Ten Commandments? How

Facing God's Law

do we react to God's law? Hang-ups? Rebellion?
The Israelites did not have a hang-up with God's
authority. They had experienced God's goodness in
their lives. At the beginning of the Ten Commandments God reminds them of His goodness: "I am the
Lord your God who brought you out of Egypt, out
of the land of slavery." God uses political imagery
here; He presents Himself to the Israelite people
as a Leader who has rescued them from their op-
pression in Egypt. Here at Mount Sinai He is saying to them: "Look, I'm your Protector and Guide,
and, as such, I'd like to make a contract with you
people. I'd like to enter into a covenant relationship
with you. I've already demonstrated that I want to
be your Ruler. Now I'd like to tell you how you
can show Me that you want to be My people." Then
God spells out the Ten Commandments as the
terms of this contract.

A Contract

Seen against the background of God's goodness as a
Ruler, the commandments no longer appear as a
"big stick." The purpose of the commandments is
to help God's people respond to Him in appropriate
ways. God, our Ruler, is saying: "The gift of obedience would please Me no end."

At first glance the commandments seem like a rather
negative gift to be giving our Ruler. Every one of
them except two begins with "You shall not." A
series of "no-no's" does not seem like a very
enthusiastic response to God's goodness. Yet, the
Ten Commandments actually leave us a lot of freedom for responding to God. They only set the
limits for our relationship with God. God is saying,
"If you go beyond these limits you have broken your
contract with Me." Any life-style, any action, any
response to God within these limits will be warmly
welcomed by Him. That makes the terms of the
contract pretty generous, doesn't it?

**Setting
Limits**

Benefits are built into this contract if its terms are kept. The primary benefit is the close relationship that it provides with God. Deuteronomy 6:2 calls this a relationship of "fear," but "warm respect" may be a better way of putting it.

Primary Benefit

There is a fringe benefit to this contract too. The fringe benefit, described in Deuteronomy 5:33, is the experience of the goodness of life. The Ten Commandments provide this fringe benefit in at least three ways:

Fringe Benefits

1. **They provide a group identity.** Each commandment begins with a "you." That "you" does not only mean "you" and "you" and "you"; it also means "all of you." The contract is a group contract. It grows out of a group movement and helps that movement to continue. The Ten Commandments provide us with a group identity when we take them seriously as a group.

2. **They help us to relate to each other.** The first four commandments are concerned mostly about our relationship with God, but the last six are concerned about how we "get on" with each other. These last six commandments help us to have happy interpersonal relationships.

3. **They build a bond between generations.** Deuteronomy 6:2 talks of passing these commandments on to "your sons and your descendants." These commandments are a heritage we share with our parents and grandparents. They are something so good that we can pass them on to our children.

Take a moment to study the three benefits of the Ten Commandments. Are there additional benefits? Circle the benefit which is most meaningful to you at this time.

Reflect

PHASE 3

Here is your first discovery group session. Here you have opportunity to discuss your ideas and feelings. Select some of the following questions to discuss in your group. Turn to page 4 for instructions.

1. Who are the authority people in your life? How do you react to them? Is your reaction to God and His law similar? Discuss.

2. What good things has God done in your life recently? Be specific. If you are not aware of God's love and goodness in your experience, the Ten Commandments and the teachings of Jesus will be a burden to you.

3. Discuss responses and answers in the personal discovery phase of this lesson.

4. If you enjoy the song "Obey My Voice" why not make it the class theme song for this quarter?

2. The Priority of God

By Glen R. Horst

Exodus 20:3-5a

You shall have no other god to set against me.

You shall not make a carved image for yourself nor the likeness of anything in the heavens above, or on the earth below, or in the waters under the earth.

You shall not bow down to them or worship them; for I, the Lord your God, am a jealous god.

Matthew 6:24-33

"No servant can be the slave of two masters; for either he will hate the first and love the second, or he will be devoted to the first and think nothing of the second. You cannot serve God and Money.

"Therefore I bid you put away anxious thoughts about food and drink to keep you alive, and clothes to cover your body. Surely life is more than food, the body more than clothes. Look at the birds of the air; they do not sow and reap and store in barns, yet your heavenly Father feeds them. You are worth more than the birds! Is there a man of you who by anxious thought can add a foot to his height? And why be anxious about clothes? Consider how the lilies grow in the fields; they do not work, they do not spin; and yet, I tell you, even Solomon in all his splendour was not attired like one of these. But if that is how God clothes the grass in the fields, which is there today, and tomorrow is thrown on the stove, will he not all the more clothe you? How little faith you have! No, do not ask anxiously, "What are we to eat? What are we to drink? What shall we wear?" All these are things for the heathen to run after, not for you, because your heavenly Father knows that you need them all. Set your mind on God's kingdom and his justice before everything else, and all the rest will come to you as well."

Hearing God's Word

1. Read Matthew 6:24-33 printed on the preceding page. Take time to relate it to your personal life. Then answer the following:

The first thing that struck me when I read this passage was (**circle one**):

    a. I am trying to serve two masters, and it doesn't work

    b. my worry is a sign that I have my values all messed up

    c. I shouldn't worry about the future

    d. I put too much importance on things

    e. none of these

    f. all of these

2. Underline ideas in Exodus 20:3-5a which are similar to the ones found in Matthew 6:24-33. Related passages to read are: Jeremiah 1:4-10; Exodus 34:11-17; Psalm 62. God speaks to you through His Word.

Pray and Reflect

Doing God's Word

If I were to take Matthew 6:24-34 seriously, it would mean (**circle one**):

    a. a radical change in my present values

    b. a radical change in my priorities

    c. a radical change in my life-style

    d. no change at all

Within the last decade some theologians have talked about the "death of God." If they are using this phrase to describe how seriously modern man takes God, then it seems they are on to something. In most areas of life man no longer seems to feel a need for God. Modern man no longer looks to God for help in making ethical decisions; nor does he consider God to be important in helping men to become whole, healthy human beings. Our society functions as though God were absent. Many would agree with Sigmund Freud that the notion of God is an illusion, and as an illusion we are better to be rid of it.

No Need for God

However, behind man's arrogance there is something else going on -- there is the endless search for something worth living for. People cannot stand the thought that maybe life is meaningless. They are looking for something that is big enough to be committed to -- something big enough to organize their lives around. Each person needs to commit his life to something, and we usually do whether we're aware of it, or not. When God is rejected as an option for commitment, He is replaced with substitutes. These substitutes are phony gods.

An Endless Search

One of the phony gods we worship is man himself. Man is worshiped in a number of ways:
1. Sex is one way of worshiping man (woman!). Cults have been built around the female body with Miss America and Miss Universe pageants. **Playboy, Penthouse,** and other magazines picture females as lambs without blemish. To be a success in our culture a person must act as though he, or she, is continually fizzing with sexual excitement.

Man: A Phony God

13

2. The intellectual powers of man are also worshiped. Science and technology are held up as demonstrations of how great man really is. When Freud suggested that we drop the notion of God, he suggested that science would take its place.

3. By worshiping society we worship man. What's the latest fashion? What do my friends think? What's everybody else doing? We have our antennae out for signals from other people to find out what they think of us and what they expect from us.

Nation:
A Phony God

Our nation is a second phony god that is worshiped in our modern world. In the United States of America worship of this god can take the form of a blind acceptance of all America stands for. "America: Love It or Leave It" is a typical slogan of the American cult of nationalism. Canadians may worship their country in the form of anti-Americanism. While some of the Canadian feelings of resentment toward the United States may be understandable, these feelings put Canadians in danger of making their country an object of ultimate loyalty.

Security:
A Phony God

A third phony god which is highly regarded in our society is security. Materialism is one form in which this god is worshiped. The more things we own the more secure and worthwhile we feel. Buying things, caring for the things we've bought, and longing for things we don't have -- these are the cultic acts of materialism.

Education is another form in which we worship the phony god, security. Education means extra dollars and job security. With overcrowded colleges and a flooded job market our worship of the god of security grows more frantic.

14

In the midst of our worship of phony gods we hear the voice of the real God speaking. He says: "You shall have no other god to set against me." God is saying to the Israelites and to us: "I know that there are other gods vying for your allegiance, but I want you to know that I am a jealous God. I want to be your God and I want to be your only God. That's the way it's got to be if you're going to have a covenant with Me." Centuries later Jesus stated this commandment another way in the Sermon on the Mount when He observed: "No servant can be the slave of two masters; for either he will hate the first and love the second, or he will be devoted to the first and think nothing of the second."

The Real God Speaks

God backs up His First Commandment with action. He has proved that He is the only God through His saving activity. Jethro, Moses' father-in-law, celebrates this saving activity when he says: "Blessed be the Lord who has saved you from the power of Egypt and of Pharaoh. Now I know that the Lord is the greatest of all gods, because he has delivered the people from the power of the Egyptians who dealt so arrogantly with them" (Ex. 18:10-12). Matthew 6:25-34 speaks of God's saving activity in another way. It talks about His willingness to look after His people in the same way He cares for the birds of the air and the lilies of the field. God is supreme -- He says so and He demonstrates it.

God Proves His Supremacy

Few would question God's supremacy. Most would say they want to be loyal to God. Yet, we are often torn between conflicting loyalties. The challenge of the First Commandment is to put God first and alone -- it is the challenge to put our allegiance to man, to nation, to security, and to whatever other phony gods we may have in second place to our allegiance to God and to His will.

The Challenge

1. T. S. Eliot in his poem, "The Hollow Men," describes men as "the hollow men . . . the stuffed men." Find this poem in an anthology and have it read in class.

How does this poem make you feel? What evidence does Eliot provide to support his view of man? Does this description describe you sometime?

2. Write a short autobiography which describes your search for something meaningful to which you can commit your life. Why not share these with each other?

3. Circle the false gods present in your life and put a check mark beside the object of your devotion.

Man: ———— worshiping sex

———— worshiping science and technologies

———— worshiping society by following fads and fashions.

Nation:

———— My country is the best. I obey its leaders in everything they ask.

Security:

———— I believe more possessions will bring happiness.

———— Receiving a college degree is my main goal in life at present.

4. Share what the real God has spoken to you in your personal discovery and in the class study and discussion.

3. More Than Lip Service

By Glen R. Horst

Exodus 20:7

You shall not make wrong use of the name of the Lord your God; the Lord will not leave unpunished the man who misuses his name.

Matthew 6:1-6

"Be careful not to make a show of your religion before men; if you do, no reward awaits you in your Father's house in heaven.

"Thus, when you do some act of charity, do not announce it with a flourish of trumpets, as the hypocrites do in synagogue and in the streets to win admiration from men. I tell you this: they have their reward already. No; when you do some act of charity, do not let your left hand know what your right is doing; your good deed must be secret, and your Father who sees what is done in secret will reward you.

"Again, when you pray, do not be like the hypocrites; they love to say their prayers standing up in synagogue and at the street-corners, for everyone to see them. I tell you this: they have their reward already. But when you pray, go into a room by yourself, shut the door, and pray to your Father who is there in the secret place; and your Father who sees what is secret will reward you."

Mark 7:5-8

Accordingly, these Pharisees and the lawyers asked him, "Why do your disciples not conform to the ancient tradition, but eat their food with defiled hands?" He answered, "Isaiah was right when he prophesied about you hypocrites in these words: 'This people pays me lip-service, but their heart is far from me: their worship of me is in vain, for they teach as doctrines the commandments of men.' You neglect the commandment of God, in order to maintain the tradition of men."

1. Read the three passages printed on the previous page and discover how they are related.

_____

_____

_____

2. Here are some ways God's name is misused. Locate the passage of Scripture in which the various misuses are described. Some passages may describe several misuses:

a. performing religious acts for man's praise —

Hearing God's Word

_____

b. pretending to be religious when you really are not _____

c. not being direct and open in your speech

_____

d. saying the right words but not doing them

_____

e. performing religious ceremony but letting social injustice abound _____

> Mark 7:1-8
> Matthew 5:33-37
> Matthew 6:1-6
> Isaiah 1:10-17
> Matthew 21:23-32

Pray and Reflect

Doing God's Word

What attitudes do you want God's Spirit to release within you?

_____

_____

_____

_____

What's in a name? Does it mean anything that my name is Glen? Or, could my name just as easily be Darcy? Or Ian? Or Delford? Or John? People really don't attach much importance to a name, do they? With our lighthearted attitude toward names it is hard for us to understand the Third Commandment. This commandment is about the importance of names. It is about the importance of one name in particular -- God's name. The Third Commandment takes God's name very seriously. That's the way it was in the Old Testament. The Old Testament people took names seriously -- not only God's name, but all names. When it was God's name they were using, they took it even that much more seriously.

What's in a Name?

In the Old Testament a name was a vital part of the person named. A name expressed the character of a man; it was an expression of a man's personality. For this reason names were sometimes changed. Remember the encounter that Jacob had with God at Peniel? (See Genesis 32.) That encounter was so significant in Jacob's life that his name was changed. He was no longer called Jacob -- his name was now Israel. The change in name represented a change in Jacob's character. In the same way God's name was seen as something which was related to His personality. God's name represented His power and His holiness. God's name represented His steadfastness and His truthfulness. When a person used God's name, he was talking about God's very nature.

A Name Says a Lot

Misusing God's Name

Since God's name was so closely tied to His personal characteristics, it is not so surprising that the Old Testament man felt that to know God's name meant to know God. To know God's name meant that you could enter into a relationship with Him. In fact, to know God's name meant that you could try to control God. If a man knew God's name, he could use it to get God's attention. A man could use God's name to back up things he said, to bless himself and his family, and to curse his enemies. This is exactly where the concern of the Third Commandment comes in.

This commandment is concerned about people trying to use God's name for their own ends. It is concerned about the misuse of the power of God's name. The Third Commandment is warning men not to use God's name to manipulate Him.

Getting God on Our Side

Today we misuse God's name in subtle ways. One of the ways we misuse it is by calling on it in support of our nationalistic civil religion. The opening prayers of those autumn football games are an example of this religion. While thousands of people stand hushed in the stadium, a clergyman prays a prayer that lumps God, country, and good sportsmanship all into one bag. Every time a clergyman is asked to open a public meeting with prayer to be followed by the national anthem, we are in danger of using God to support our public causes and our country. Remembrance Day services in the autumn around war memorials can also serve as expressions of a nationalistic religious spirit. In other settings politicians capitalize on our nationalistic religious spirit by using God's name for their own ends. They use it as evidence of personal integrity and as a way to enhance political prestige.

Christians misuse God's name when acts of service, done in God's name, become ways of building prestige. Jesus, in Matthew 6, calls this kind of thing hypocrisy. Hypocrisy is a person seeming to do an act of service because of his love for God, but, in fact, doing it because of his desire for recognition. I know well the hurt that comes when no one offers a word of appreciation for my efforts. Yet, such hurt is a signal for me to take a sharp look at my motivation for doing a thing. Am I putting my heart into something because of my relationship of love and acceptance with God, or am I involved because I am on a personal ego trip?

Using God for an Ego Trip

Pious words may be used to hide our insincerity in life-style. Do we do a lot of talking to conceal our lack of obedience? Do we separate our Christian beliefs from our actions? If so, we are guilty of an insincere life-style. We may also be insincere in our worship. When we continue to use dull and empty worship forms because they are part of our church's tradition, we are concealing the emptiness of our experience with God by calling on His name.

Hiding Insincerity

Are you surprised that no mention has been made of using God's name as a cussword? The usual interpretation of the Third Commandment is that it forbids profanity. This is not a wrong interpretation. God's name is not to be used as a cussword. Such a use is a too lighthearted way to handle it. To use God's name as a cussword is to miss the deep significance of God's name as a revelation of His power and holiness. However, let's remember that at its deepest level the Third Commandment is a forceful reminder that the Christian life is more than lip service.

God's Name as a Cussword

PHASE 3

1. Have each person in your discovery group write the answer to the following questions on paper:

> "What is the most important Christian belief for me?"
> "When is the last time I acted on this belief?"
> "How much difference does this belief make in my life?"

_____

_____

_____

_____

_____

2. Identify your attitude toward the following religious experiences. Add experiences not listed.

> Personal Bible reading and prayer
> Participation in public worship
> Singing in the congregation
> Fellowship in your youth group
> A walk in the woods on a sunny day

_____

_____

_____

_____

3. Identify areas in your life where you are serving for the recognition you get. Whom are you trying to impress? Yourself? Your friends? Your parents? Teachers? God?

4. Work, Rest, and Worship

By Laurence Martin

Exodus 20:8-11

Remember to keep the sabbath day holy. You have six days to labour and do all your work. But the seventh day is a sabbath of the Lord your God; that day you shall not do any work, you, your son or your daughter, your slave or your slave-girl, your cattle or the alien within your gates; for in six days the Lord made heaven and earth, the sea, and all that is in them, and on the seventh day he rested. Therefore the Lord blessed the sabbath day and declared it holy.

Mark 2:23-28

One Sabbath he was going through the cornfields; and his disciples, as they went, began to pluck ears of corn. The Pharisees said to him, "Look, why are they doing what is forbidden on the Sabbath?" He answered, "Have you never read what David did when he and his men were hungry and had nothing to eat? He went into the House of God, in the time of Abiathar the High Priest, and ate the sacred bread, though no one but a priest is allowed to eat it, and even gave it to his men."

He also said to them, "The Sabbath was made for the sake of man and not man for the Sabbath: therefore the Son of Man is sovereign even over the Sabbath."

Luke 4:16-19

So he came to Nazareth, where he had been brought up, and went to synagogue on the Sabbath day as he regularly did. He stood up to read the lesson and was handed the scroll of the prophet Isaiah. He opened the scroll and found the passage which says,

"The Spirit of the Lord is upon me because he has anointed me;
he has sent me to announce good news to the poor,
to proclaim release for prisoners and recovery of sight for the blind;
to let the broken victims go free,
to proclaim the year of the Lord's favour."

1. Read Exodus 20:8-11. How were God's people to observe the Sabbath day?

_____

_____

To whom did the law apply?

_____

_____

Hearing God's Word

2. Read Romans 7:1-6, 21-25. What kind of slavery is described? _____

_____

Identify the mood of the passage.

_____

Read Romans 8:1-4 and discover how a person can be freed from spiritual slavery. _____

_____

3. Hebrews 10:19-25 is a description of worship. What personal acts of worship are described? What social acts of worship are mentioned? Suggest ways to facilitate similar experiences in your church life.

Pray and Reflect

Festival _____ Remember_____ Rest _____
Renewal _____ Direction _____ Reflect_____
What mental image does each word create in your mind?

My idea of a meaningful Sunday is _____

_____

_____

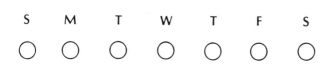

S   M   T   W   T   F   S

Take a pencil, crayon, or felt tip pen and decorate each circle indicating how you feel about each day of the week. What makes some days more meaningful than others? How did you indicate some days are more important than others? Discuss your responses with class members.

Color Me Joyful

In the eyes of God all days are good. Romans 14: 5 ff. Would you like to perform the same activities each day of the week? Of course not! All of us need the opportunity to change the pace of living, to think and to reflect and to dream of the future. In the Genesis account of creation (Genesis 2:1-3) the worth of creative activity is highlighted. God was reflecting upon His works of creation and enjoying them. Was He perhaps celebrating the glory of His creation? The Book of Job says that the sons of God shouted for joy during the creation of the earth. Job 38:7. Take time today to think about and celebrate the creative work you have done recently.

Celebrate Creative Acts

1. What are some of the creative things you accomplished this past week?

_____

_____

2. How do you feel after performing a creative activity or project -- something which reflects your personal thinking and skill?

Reflect and Plan

_____

What are some of the things you must do this coming week? Remember that when you are being creative for good you are participating in God's will for this world.

_____

_____

_____

_____

Celebrate Freedom and Salvation

In Deuteronomy 5:15 there is another reason to keep the Sabbath day special. This passage indicates that God's people were to remember that they were slaves in Egypt and God, through their leader Moses, helped them escape and become free people. That is something to sing about, shout about, and to remember. Well! Use the seventh day of every week to remember that God helped you to become free people. Free from slavery, free to worship and serve King Yahweh rather than Pharaoh. Free to possess land and become God's people.

Reflect and Discuss

Who is a slave today? Have you ever felt like a slave -- that other people control your life? There is also a real kind of spiritual slavery. Do you want to remain free and stay that way? Paul speaks of being a slave to personal passions and appetites as well as being a slave to the devil. (See Romans 7:1-6, 21-25; 8:1-4.)

Members of the early Christian movement made the transition from the Sabbath to Sunday. 1 Corinthians 16:2. The resurrection of Jesus Christ was the new creative act of God resulting in a new creation of people obedient to Jesus Christ. God had broken through the barriers and limitations of the old creation and a new order, a new age began. The early followers of Jesus received the power of the Holy Spirit and were freed from the power of fear, of sin, and of selfishness. For the early Christians the day of the new creation and of freedom from slavery was the day of resurrection.

The New Creation -- A New Age

The Sabbath (Sunday in the Christian tradition) is not intended to become a new form of slavery -- a slavery to do's and don'ts. Rather the Sabbath was designed to benefit mankind. Indeed all of God's laws reflect the wisdom of God for the welfare of the human family. Study Mark 2:23-28.

The Sabbath Is for Man

Discovering Creative Ways to Celebrate Sunday

The Sunday Drivers' Cheer
(to the tune of "On Wisconsin")

On you drivers!
On you drivers!
Inch your way along!
Heading for a Sunday outing—
Fifty million strong (*Stop honking!*)

See them lined up—
We will wind up
Home at 10 o'clock!
And to think we only drove
A-round the block!

*"The Sunday Drivers' Cheer" from **The Mad Morality,** publisher William M. Gaines, **Mad** Magazine. © 1973 by E. C. Publications, Inc.

1. Is Sunday a festival occasion in your church home? Are you resurrected to new power and vision or is Sunday as solemn as a funeral procession? Review the elements mentioned in this lesson which could help in making Sunday (Sabbath observance) truly a religious festive occasion.

3. What kind of activities help you reflect upon the meaning of life and aid in discovering a vision of who you are to become?

4. What activities do you think are appropriate for a Christian on Sunday if you:
> -- live in the inner city?
> -- are a dairy farmer?
> -- work in an office all week?
> -- go to school five days a week?

What does the principle "the Sabbath was made for man" mean in making practical decisions?

PHASE 3

1. "To be creative for good is doing God's will in life." Take time to share with your discovery group some of your creative achievements. Comment on each other's gifts and abilities. How can you make this experience truly festive?

2. Each group should develop a definition of leisure. Fill in the following sentence: Leisure is ——————————.

3. As a result of this lesson I ——————————

5. What's Good About the Past?

By Ross T. Bender

Exodus 20:12

Honour your father and your mother, that you may live long in the land which the Lord your God is giving you.

Deuteronomy 6:6-9

These commandments which I give you this day are to be kept in your heart; you shall repeat them to your sons, and speak of them indoors and out of doors, when you lie down and when you rise. Bind them as a sign on the hand and wear them as a phylactery on the forehead; write them up on the doorposts of your houses and on your gates.

Ephesians 6:1-4

Children, obey your parents, for it is right that you should. "Honour your father and mother" is the first commandment with a promise attached, in the words: "that it may be well with you and that you may live long in the land."

You fathers, again, must not goad your children to resentment, but give them the instruction, and the correction, which belong to a Christian upbringing.

2 Timothy 1:5

I am reminded of the sincerity of your faith, a faith which was alive in Lois your grandmother and Eunice your mother before you, and which, I am confident, lives in you also.

1. As you read the listed passages discover the acts of God in the Hebrew-Christian tradition and how they were to be communicated.

Deuteronomy 26:1-11 _____

_____

Deuteronomy 6:4-9 _____

_____

Psalm 78:1-8 _____

_____

Acts 2:29-39 _____

_____

Pray and Reflect

Close your eyes and remember. Picture Abraham, Sarah, Jacob, Moses, Ruth, David, and others in your mind. Imagine what kind of persons they were. These people are your relatives by faith. Their story is part of your story. Identify your feelings and new insights which you have.

PHASE 2

Red Guard Mennos

The recent "Cultural Revolution" in the People's Republic of China was an attempt by the ruling party to wipe out traditional Chinese culture through such means as burning the libraries which contained the record of that heritage. Large bands of Chinese youth known as the Red Guard participated enthusiastically in this wanton destruction until their elders recognized the folly of the attempt and put an end to it. Most North American youth are not engaged in this kind of hostile reaction to their past. However, some couldn't care less about their history and others are rejecting it outright. They view it as a burden to be borne instead of an inheritance to be gained. Even some Christian youth are reacting vigorously to what they consider the backwardness or hypocrisy of their elders. They express it by open criticism or deviant behavior which is shocking to their parents.

What's good about the past? they want to know. The record of history, even our church history, makes for dreary reading. Not so much that it is dull but that it is filled with stories of church fights and splits among brethren. They called it standing for principles but looking at it from a distance, it seems more like stubborn and rigid personalities insisting on getting their own way. Today we don't want other people telling us what to do. Everybody should be free to do his own thing without anyone leaning on him. We are only interested in the here and now. Here and now is where the action is! Don't tell me about "Once upon a time" and "Long, long ago." The church isn't relevant because it buries its head in the sands of the past and the eternal. It is like the fellow who was so heavenly minded that he was no earthly good. The church should get involved in the issues of our day and stop looking backward and forward.

Long, Long Ago

The problem with this argument, which sounds so persuasive at first, is that it gives us no way to measure what is relevant. How can we make a judgment about what is going on in the here and now if we live only within the here and now? Once I was sitting in a train waiting for it to leave the station. For a few minutes I thought we were moving, but it turned out that it was the train beside us moving in the opposite direction. Had I glanced out the other side I would have seen my train was standing still. We need the perspective of seeing out both windows to measure our movement. To live only in the here and now is to live in a box with no windows at all. We need the windows of our history, both good and bad, to know where we are headed today and what kind of progress, if any, we are making.

Windows

In the **Fiddler on the Roof**, Tevye says, "Because of our traditions, everyone knows who he is and what God expects him to do. . . . Without our traditions our lives would be as shaky as a fiddler on the roof." The theme of this drama is the role of tradition in providing stability for the Jewish people. Tevye's security is sorely tested when each of his three daughters in turn marries without his help and counsel. When his third daughter is married in a Russian Orthodox ceremony to a non-Jew, Tevye is torn between his religious beliefs and his love for his daughter. In the midst of his vacillation he finally concludes that he can bend his traditional beliefs no farther and considers his daughter dead. The agony of change is dramatically portrayed in this conflict when the old gives way to the new. Both Tevye and Chava, his daughter, suffered; he did not want to offend his God and she did not want to hurt her father.

Although Tevye is deeply rooted in the tradition which has shaped him, he no longer remembers where that tradition all began. Nor is he able to sort out what in it was God's unchanging will and what was added by men throughout the years. The Jewish tradition began in the call of Abraham and the exodus of slaves from Egypt under Moses' leadership. God prepared the way and led those who were "no people" across the Red Sea through the wilderness to the foot of Mt. Sinai. There He gave them an identity as God's own people and entered into covenant relationship with them. In Deuteronomy 6 we hear the story of His deliverance repeated, and the command to pass on the heritage of faith from the fathers to the sons. No opportunity was lost to teach them diligently the gracious acts of God as well as God's requirement to love Him absolutely and one's neighbor as oneself.

From "No People" to "God's People"

We, too, draw upon our history in order to understand who we are. We answer the question in various ways. We are people of a particular tribe: Swiss, German, Dutch, Russian, Spanish, African, Asian. We are people of a particular status: well-to-do, comfortably middle-class or trying to be. We are people with particular political loyalties: Canadians or Americans, Liberals or Progressive Conservatives, Democrats or Republicans. Our national birthday parties cause us to ask, "Where did we come from? Who are we now? and Where are we going?" Who are the heroes from our history (the prophets or the politicians?), and with whom do we identify as we decide where we belong and to what we are committed? **Those who belong to the people of God may carry the passports of the nations of this world, but they are first of all members of a kingdom that leaps over all borders between the nations and includes persons from all tribes and peoples and tongues.**

Who Are We?

1. **Fiddler on the Roof** raises the question, "What's good about the past?" Those who have read the book or seen the dramatic production on stage or screen should discuss the way in which the basic theme is developed.

2. Merle Good's play, **These People Mine,** presents a similar theme in a very effective way. Have you seen it or read the paperback? What was your reaction?

3. Use the Sunday school hour for a walking tour through the cemetery. If you are planning intergenerational classes divide the class into "tour groups" of 3 to 5 persons composed of people representing each of the generations in your congregation. As you recall the names and history of the past, compare the church you attend today to the church of a century ago, the church of your grandparents, and the church of your parents. Compare all three periods to the church in the New Testament.

4. Some young men have refused to cooperate with Selective Service by failing to register for the draft. They have insisted that in so doing they are only following to its logical conclusion what the church has taught them about an absolute allegiance to God. Do you agree?

5. As a result of this lesson I am going to

_____

_____

_____

6. How Important Is Life?

By Warner Jackson

Exodus 20:13

You shall not commit murder.

Matthew 5:21-26

"You have learned that our forefathers were told, 'Do not commit murder; anyone who commits murder must be brought to judgement.' But what I tell you is this: Anyone who nurses anger against his brother must be brought to judgement. If he abuses his brother he must answer for it to the court; if he sneers at him he will have to answer for it in the fires of hell.

"If, when you are bringing your gift to the altar, you suddenly remember that your brother has a grievance against you, leave your gift where it is before the altar. First go and make your peace with your brother, and only then come back and offer your gift.

"If someone sues you, come to terms with him promptly while you are both on your way to court; otherwise he may hand you over to the judge, and the judge to the constable, and you will be put in jail. I tell you, once you are there you will not be let out till you have paid the last farthing."

James 4:1, 2b

What causes conflicts and quarrels among you? Do they not spring from the aggressiveness of your bodily desires? You want something which you cannot have, and so you are bent on murder; you are envious, and cannot attain your ambition, and so you quarrel and fight.

1 John 3:15-18

For everyone who hates his brother is a murderer, and no murderer, as you know, has eternal life dwelling within him. It is by this that we know what love is: that Christ laid down his life for us. And we in our turn are bound to lay down our lives for our brothers. But if a man has enough to live on, and yet when he sees his brother in need shuts up his heart against him, how can it be said that the divine love dwells in him?

My children, love must not be a matter of words or talk; it must be genuine, and show itself in action.

PHASE 1

Read Exodus 20:13 and Matthew 5:21-24 and think about the meaning of the words for your life. Then answer the following questions:

1. Murder is defined in the Scripture passage as (**circle one**):
   a. killing your brother

   b. slandering your brother to others

   c. tearing down your brother's self-worth

   d. making it difficult for your brother

   e. not giving in to your brother

2. According to the passage, God expects (**circle one**):
   a. the person who has done wrong to go to God and make it right

   b. the person who has been wronged to go to God and make it right

   c. the person who has done wrong to go to the person and make it right

   d. the person who has been wronged to go the person and make it right

3. Jot down in the space below the names of the people with whom you live at the moment. Then, beside each name, place the letter which describes your present relationship.

_____
_____
_____
_____

a. Our relationship is half-affirming. I try to build up this person but he refuses to build me up.

b. Our relationship is completely affirming. I build up this person and he builds me up. We enable each other to be our best selves.

c. Our relationship is half-affirming in the other direction. This person tries to build me up, but I do not know how to build him up.

d. Our relationship is mutually destructive. I tear down this person's self-worth and he tears down my self-worth. We are destroying each other.

A right to a claim demand or expectation that will be protected by law. Many laws exist prescribing the right not to be deprived of life without due process of law. The "right" to life is a demand which the law will respect, at least in North America. This means that if the "right" to life is violated, or jeopardized, the law should provide a remedy. In North America a "reverence for life" exists on paper, at least. Nevertheless, there are some shocking abuses against life today which cause us to ask whether there is in fact a "right to life."

The Right to Life

Do we reverence life when a patient lacking money must die because he cannot afford a kidney machine? Would not the "right" to life carry with it a right to live in a neighborhood which is neither overcrowded with people nor have substandard rat-infested dwelling units tolerated by government? The world in tolerating a known killer such as drug abuse does not appear to reverence life. Weak and ineffective law enforcement which encourages the convicted criminal to repeat his crime does not clearly reveal "a reverence for life." We are polluting the air through the luxury of the automobile. Industry continues polluting the water so that the very environment upon which life depends is being destroyed. Chemical preservatives in foods are thought to be a menace to health and to life. Greed and the pursuit of money is often put first. Just how much do we reverence life? No wonder some people talk about a "right" to medicare, a "right" to decent housing, a duty of government to stop polluters, to arrest the drug traffic, to get tough with criminals.

Is the "Right" Denied?

**To Die
for Life**

How much do we really reverence life? Jesus taught the necessity to "die" as the road to life everlasting, to hate one's life in this world, to deny self in order to find "eternal life." The person who truly values life is called upon to sacrifice selfish pursuits in order to preserve, perpetuate, and save his life and to enjoy it more abundantly. Jesus Christ came to give true life. John 10:10. True life, Jesus taught, consists not in the abundance of things a man possesses.

Discuss

Of what then does true life consist? What do you consider to be the good life?

**Love and
Life**

The Word tells us that "God is love." 1 John 4:8, 16. All persons reborn by the Spirit of God are His children and acquire God's nature -- a capacity to love. Romans 5:5. "He that loveth not knoweth not God. . . ." Love will move us to suffer abuse. Love will move us to work no ill to another. Romans 13. The identifying mark of a true believer in Christ is whether he loves or not. This is God's love in us which acts out of a good will to all without discrimination or partiality. This love may be stifled. Christians not yet perfect in love (1 John 4) are called upon to grow up in Christ to be perfect (2 Peter 1:4 ff.) which is "charity," the greatest virtue of all (1 Corinthians 13). Love requires a conscientious opposition to war as well as against economic, social, and political exploitation of others.

Love requires patience with others, forgiveness of their offenses against us, and a tolerance of their views. War, social violence, and unfair ridicule or taking unfair advantage of another person in any way is not how "love" behaves. "Whosoever hateth his brother is a murderer; and ye know that no murderer hath eternal life abiding in him."

There are many forces today which when unleashed destroy life. Take a moment to imagine you are involved in the following:

-- A member of your family has been killed by a drunken driver.

-- A child about to be born has a chance of being grossly deformed. Abortion is one solution open to you.

-- As parents you are constantly tempted to use your superior knowledge and power to discipline and influence your child.

-- A doctor needs to make a decision whether to use the latest in medical technology to prolong the life of a person suffering from a terminal disease.

-- The turmoil of a person so depressed by failure and guilt that suicide seems the only answer.

-- The struggles of a prison warden faced with the task of rehabilitating violent men and women.

These are only some of the questions to which this lesson speaks. What additional situations can you suggest?

PHASE 3

1. Take time in your discovery group to share the answers to Phase One.

2. If your discovery group wants to have an additional Bible study as a group, read 1 Corinthians 13 and discover the qualities of love which promote reverence for life.

Qualities of Love	Do I possess them?			
1 Corinthians 13	Yes	Usually	Sometimes	No

3. Some discovery group activities are:

-- Visit your local court and follow a criminal trial through to its conclusion to see what happens to convicted criminals.

-- Write your provincial or state government to find out what is happening in the area of pollution control.

-- Contact local representatives in government to discover what steps are being taken to provide medical aid to the poor.

-- Ask your local Mutual Aid representative to explain the benefits it offers to the brotherhood.

-- Learn about the church agencies in existence which help the Christian to serve his fellowman.

7. A Christian View of Sex

By Ed and Helen Alderfer

Exodus 20:14

You shall not commit adultery.

Matthew 5:27, 28

"You have learned that they were told, 'Do not commit adultery.' But what I tell you is this: If a man looks on a woman with a lustful eye, he has already committed adultery with her in his heart."

1 Corinthians 6:13b-20

But it is not true that the body is for lust; it is for the Lord — and the Lord for the body. God not only raised our Lord from the dead; he will also raise us by his power. Do you not know that your bodies are limbs and organs of Christ? Shall I then take from Christ his bodily parts and make them over to a harlot? Never! You surely know that anyone who links himself with a harlot becomes physically one with her (for Scripture says, "The pair shall become one flesh"); but he who links himself with Christ is one with him, spiritually. Shun fornication. Every other sin that a man can commit is outside the body; but the fornicator sins against his own body. Do you not know that your body is a shrine of the indwelling Holy Spirit, and the Spirit is God's gift to you? You do not belong to yourselves; you were bought at a price. Then honour God in your body.

PHASE 1

Read carefully Matthew 5:27-29, 38, 39, 43-45. Jesus is spelling out in clear terms some standards of behavior.

1. The common thread that runs through all three paragraphs is (**circle one**):
   - a. a new measurement for judging Christian behavior
   - b. a radical new pattern for developing a Christian life-style
   - c. a new focus for forming Christian relationships

2. The difference in the concept of love as portrayed by Jesus and the one portrayed by Hollywood is (**circle one**):
   - a. one is all giving, the other is all getting
   - b. one is enabling persons, the other is disabling them
   - c. one sees others as persons, the other sees people as things
   - d. one is costly in terms of commitment, the other is not

3. When I think of the sexual act, I think of (**rank 1 to 3 in order of significance**):
   - ____ physical pleasure
   - ____ a personal relationship
   - ____ a lifetime commitment

4. In my opinion, the best way to deal with lust is (**circle one**):
   - a. repress it (deny it)
   - b. suppress it (force it under)
   - c. confess it (admit it)
   - d. overcome it (fight it)
   - e. rechannel it (sublimate it)
   - f. express it (do it)

Pray and Reflect

1. Of the three paragraphs in the Matthew passages the hardest one for me to live is (**rank 1 to 3 in order of difficulty**):
   - ____ the other sex
   - ____ the other cheek
   - ____ the other side

2. If I am going to do something about the area that is causing me the greatest problem, I must start out by (**finish the sentence**):

Sex is the answer someone gave your parents when you were born and they asked, "Is it a boy or a girl?"

Sex is 36-24-36.

Sex is a certain feeling that you get (if you're a girl) when you find a boy isn't someone to "hate" but someone special because he is a boy. (Adapt that sentence if you're a boy.)

What Is Sex?

Sex can make you feel good or bad. It can frighten you or comfort you.

Sex is the birds and the bees and the flowers and a lot more.

Sex is designed by God -- "Male and female he created them...."

"Stop," you say, "I didn't know it was all right to talk about sex. My parents never tell me anything. The word 'sex' is a 'no-no' in our church."

Who's Silent About Sex?

And parents say, "When we try to talk to our teenagers they clam up, as though we don't know anything."

Is it a conspiracy? Who started the idea that talking about sex isn't nice?

Why not talk about it? Is it evil? No. Nothing could be further from God's plan for it. He made men and women sexual beings and said that it was "very good." Later He came into the world and chose to come in the form of a body, His Son's. Just because there are indecent pictures in the boys' locker room and off-color words scrawled on the walls of both boys' and girls' rest rooms does not mean that sex is bad. Just because some people whisper about it doesn't mean that it isn't good. St. Augustine wrote, "Why should I be ashamed to speak of that which it pleased Almighty God to create?"

Is Sex Evil?

"In the image of God he created him; male and female he created them." And being in His image includes the capacity to love, to care deeply for others, and to hunt for ways to help and not hurt each other. In Arthur Miller's play **Death of a Salesman** the main character is Willy Loman, a traveling salesman and a pathetic sort of man. His son, Biff, a high school, athletic hero who has gotten into trouble, goes to Boston to find his father to ask him for help. There he catches his father in an act of adultery with a strange woman in a hotel room. Seeing his son's shock, Willy tells him, "She's nothing to me, Biff. I was lonely, I was terribly lonely."

Willy Loman's personal needs were so great that they drove him to use another person to try to fill them.

In the Image of God -- Me?

The Bible gives many rules about sex. Behind them are the great truths from which they come. Once when Jesus was asked which was the greatest commandment in the law He said, " 'Thou shalt love the Lord thy God with all thy heart, and with all thy soul, and with all thy mind.' This is the first and great commandment. And the second is like unto it, 'Thou shalt love thy neighbour as thyself.' " It is hard to imagine that anyone who would live by those great commandments would not know how to use sex rightly.

Apply the description of love in 1 Corinthians 13. Test it against a friendship you have:

The Bible Has Guidelines

Is it too idealistic?
Does it feel "right"?
Does it act responsibly?
Does it fit the poet's description of love as "a many-splendored thing"?

Study and Discuss

Whether there seems to be a ban on talking about sex where you live or whether it is out in the open, there are some questions and answers going around. They are not regional. They can be heard in any part of the country:

Have You Heard Any of These?

Just be careful that you don't get caught.

I want what I want when I want it.

Sex is good recreation. (**Playboy** perspective.)

Can you be popular if you don't go all the way?

If sex is so good and normal why are so many people (especially parents) so edgy about it?

What Are the Options for Sexual Behavior?

Everyone has to deal with such questions and answers. Everyone has to come to some decisions about sexual behavior. Deciding not to make any decision is also a kind of decision.

The options can be broken down into four:

1. Refuse to see that there is a struggle.

Live casually and block out anything difficult.

2. Take a set of firm rules and live by them.

3. Do whatever "love" tells you to do. Let it be the one deciding factor.

4. Take a combination of 2 and 3 — love for persons and a set of moral rules for guidance.

"The negativity of the commandments marks off small areas into which free men ought not go -- precisely so that they can remain free to roam anywhere else in the great wide world."*

To Think About

*From **The Mad Morality**, by Vernard Eller, Abingdon Press, page 8. Used by permission.

PHASE 3

1. Have two persons in the discovery group take the parts of Jim and Joe and read them out loud.

Jim (who is 18): I'm tired of hearing nothing but "don'ts." I go along with Paul that love doesn't hurt people.

Joe (who is 40): Do you mean that love always knows what's best?

Jim: Yeah, that's what I mean.

Joe: Well, I'd have to say that I didn't understand myself sometimes.

Jim: What do you mean?

Joe: Sometimes when I thought I was really caring about somebody else, I was mostly just looking out for myself.

Jim: When did you decide all this?

Joe: Often not until afterward.

Jim: So you think I'm going to make a lot of mistakes?

Joe: Yes, I think you will. But I believe you will have help to make fewer if you use the "Do nots."

Jim: But. . . .

What do you think Jim was about to say? Carry the conversation on.

2. Share the results of your personal study in Phase One in the discovery group. Help each other to develop stronger convictions and clarify doubts.

8. An Owner's Rights and Responsibilities

By Warner Jackson

Exodus 20:15

You shall not steal.

Amos 8:4-6

Listen to this, you who grind the destitute and plunder the humble, you who say, "When will the new moon be over so that we may sell corn? When will the sabbath be past so that we may open our wheat again, giving short measure in the bushel and taking overweight in the silver, tilting the scales fraudulently, and selling the dust of the wheat; that we may buy the poor for silver and the destitute for a pair of shoes?"

Luke 19:1-10

Entering Jericho he made his way through the city. There was a man there named Zacchaeus; he was superintendent of taxes and very rich. He was eager to see what Jesus looked like; but, being a little man, he could not see him for the crowd. So he ran on ahead and climbed a sycomore-tree in order to see him, for he was to pass that way. When Jesus came to the place, he looked up and said, "Zacchaeus, be quick and come down; I must come and stay with you today." He climbed down as fast as he could and welcomed him gladly. At this there was a general murmur of disapproval. "He has gone in," they said, "to be the guest of a sinner." But Zacchaeus stood there and said to the Lord, "Here and now, sir, I give half my possessions to charity; and if I have cheated anyone, I am ready to repay him four times over." Jesus said to him, "Salvation has come to this house today! -- for this man too is a son of Abraham, and the Son of Man has come to seek and save what is lost."

1. Read the three passages on the previous page. Stealing is defined in these passages as (**circle answers which apply**):

a. using position of power to take advantage of poor

b. cheating in selling produce

c. taking from the rich to feed the poor

d. charging high rates of interest

Hearing God's Word

2. Read Ephesians 4:28-32 and compare it with Luke 19:1-10. What Christlike qualities become evident when a selfish person who steals accepts Jesus as Lord and Savior?

_____

_____

3. Read the story in 1 Kings 21:1-26. If you were rewriting the story to fit events and people in today's world who might the following characters and institutions represent?

Naboth _____

King Ahab _____

Queen Jezebel _____

Elders and nobles _____

Hired scoundrels _____

Elijah _____

4. Write a short story about events today where innocent people are exploited. Your class may want to submit a story to your church's youth paper for publication.

Doing God's Word

My encounter with the Word of God has challenged me to _____

_____

_____

"Thou shalt not steal" is designed by God to establish and to preserve a proper regard for personhood and ownership. Stealing is the unlawful taking and carrying away anything of value belonging to another with intent to steal the same. The Apostle Paul insisted that **love** of the kind which was in Christ Jesus will move us to respect the personhood and ownership rights of others since "love worketh no ill to his neighbour" (Rom. 13:10, KJV). Love is the fulfilling of the law of God.

Stealing and Its Remedy

Men in trusted positions are accused of stealing or embezzling money from the company they work for. Young men steal automobiles and are criminally prosecuted for operating an auto without the owner's consent. Innocent persons are sometimes kidnapped by criminals for profit. Employees can cheat by loafing. Boys pluck fruit from a neighbor's tree or tomatoes from his garden. The drug pusher steals health and life for profit, from unsuspecting thrill-seeking, gullible youth.

Forms of Larceny

Theft and cheating has become so widespread until it is difficult for the law to impose effective controls. Great chain supermarkets cheat customers by selling meats with too much fat or else the weight is less than indicated on the labels. A totally new field of "rights" are rising in the legal field, called "consumer rights." All such rights are spearheaded by consumer protection leaders seeking to protect the public from being cheated. There is a great outcry against merchants who fail to give the consumer his money's worth for purchases. Money is property also, and it may be misused, lost, stolen, or forfeited. Theft is also clearly seen in the cases in which used car dealers may sell the "klunker" or "junker" as is! The usual warranties or guar-

Consumer Rights

antees that a car is fit and safe for use on the public highway is not always applied to used cars. Even some new cars sold must be recalled in order for the manufacturer to replace defective parts. Such unsafe defective vehicles are threats to the property of others when put on public roads. All such practices are modern forms of the disregard for property or the theft of the money of others without giving a fair exchange. "Thou shalt not steal."

Breach of Warranties

High interest rates paid by some debtors to creditors, is also a form of theft. Repossession of property from a debtor by a creditor is in some cases a highly unfair creditor's remedy. Especially is this true, for example, in situations in which a hardworking low-income laborer buying a car, house, or home appliance is in arrears **one** payment after the property is almost paid for. At which time the creditor unmercifully takes measures to repossess the article. This is an improper disregard by the creditor for ownership.

More on Debtors and Creditors

The landlord suffers, too. As does the tenant. A landlord ought to repair his run-down substandard property. The tenant, likewise, ought to pay rent and care for and seek to maintain the property of another while living in it.

Landlord -- Tenant

God created man. He has claims of ownership because He created us. Christ paid the price by His precious blood to redeem us from a sinful life. We are not our own. Christ has claims of ownership upon us because He bought us and is now our resurrected Lord. It is not a proper regard for the divine ownership if any person takes his life, resources, time, or talent and acts in such a manner as will suggest to the world that God Himself has no claims upon these.

The Master's Claim

The words, "Thou shalt not steal" must be considered as applying to what we call the "stewardship" of our time, talents, lives, and money. It is **sin** to "unlawfully take and carry away" ourselves, our time, talents, or money which are God's.

As you have read this lesson, what are the issues on which the commandment "Thou shall not steal" focuses?

___Is the possession of property the sacred right of every person? How much property is necessary for an individual to possess?

___How do some employers rob from employees -- which has an enslaving effect?

___How do some employees steal from their employers?

___It is reported that some supermarkets in inner-city settings take advantage of residents by charging unfair prices because they are unable to shop around for better values.

___Has the foreign policy of Canada or United States in any way robbed poorer countries of resources in the past? What about today?

___What about the policy of some companies to repossess property from a debtor by a creditor?

___Are you aware of extremely high interest rates being charged which bind people in a kind of economic slavery?

1. Here are some possible projects for discovery group activities:

-- Write to the county welfare agency inquiring about the eligibility to qualify as a recipient, and the specific details of the programs. Discuss your findings. Is the welfare program justified by a realistic human need?

-- Discuss ways citizens can fight the crime of stealing.

-- Prison reformers argue that prisons do not rehabilitate thieves. Rather, men grow worse because of the exposure to hardened criminal elements in prison. What are prison conditions like in your area? Research some of the prison rehabilitation experiments taking place. Are there ways you can become involved in helping youth who are in trouble with the law?

2. **True or False**

_____ A. Stealing can be corrected by stronger laws.

_____ B. Even love is not strong enough to defeat the selfishness which drives men to steal.

_____ C. Men always steal out of purely selfish motives.

_____ D. A true Christian never steals anything from God.

_____ E. Our time, talents, and property are our own and we may use, enjoy, or dispose of them as we see fit.

_____ F. The true Christian loves and he cannot be guilty of stealing.

3. Discuss the following story in light of today's lesson.

It is reported by Paul Martin, missionary in British Honduras: "An incident occurred in the little Maya village of San Felipe where Christians gather to fellowship in a thatched roof church building. One day while sharing with them, the conversation turned to the struggle of making a living. I asked them, 'How did you make a living before you were Christians?' One said, 'It was easy -- if things got tight we stole, made rum, or added extra hours to our time if we had a job. Now we can't do that; we don't want to do it, because we are Christians, but our children suffer and it is hard.' "

4. Share the results of personal study and commitments made in Phase One.

9. Does It Hurt to Lie?

By Warner Jackson

Exodus 20:16

You shall not give false evidence against your neighbour.

Acts 5:1-11

But there was another man, called Ananias, with his wife Sapphira, who sold a property. With the full knowledge of his wife he kept back part of the purchase-money, and part he brought and laid at the apostles' feet. But Peter said, "Ananias, how was it that Satan so possessed your mind that you lied to the Holy Spirit, and kept back part of the price of the land? While it remained, did it not remain yours? When it turned into money, was it not still at your own disposal? What made you think of doing this thing? You have lied not to men but to God." When Ananias heard these words he dropped dead; and all the others who heard were awestruck. The younger men rose and covered his body, then carried him out and buried him.

About three hours passed, and then his wife came in, unaware of what had happened. Peter turned to her and said, "Tell me, were you paid such and such a price for the land?" "Yes," she said, "that was the price." Then Peter said, "Why did you both conspire to put the Spirit of the Lord to the test? Hark! there at the door are the footsteps of those who buried your husband; and they will carry you away." And suddenly she dropped dead at his feet. When the young men came in, they found her dead; and they carried her out and buried her beside her husband. And a great awe fell upon the whole church, and upon all who heard of these events.

Ephesians 4:25

Then throw off falsehood; speak the truth to each other, for all of us are the parts of one body.

1. Read James 3:1-12 and think of your own experiences in life. Circle the illustrations about the tongue
that communicated to you most forcefully.

a. A bit in a horse's mouth.

Hearing God's Word

b. A rudder on a ship.
c. A spark starting a forest fire.
d. Comparing the tongue to wild beasts.
e. Does springwater come from the same fountain
as polluted water?
f. Can a fig tree yield olives or a grapevine figs?
g. Saltwater cannot give fresh water.

2. In the space provided, summarize the meaning of
each illustration.

3. If you like to do cartoon drawings illustrate the
figures suggested by James 3:1-12.

4. What forms of falsehood are mentioned in these
passages of Scripture: Exodus 20:16; Exodus 23:1-3?

Pray and Reflect

"Words are the media through which personalities
confront each other."

Doing God's Word

Have these passages brought to light falsehood in
your life? If so, what do you plan to do about it?

Suppose your brother is hiding in your house. A man who is chasing him with a gun asks you if your brother is there. What would you do? Tell him the truth? Or, would you feel in light of your duty to your brother you should tell the untruth? Most people likely agree it is best to tell the truth. But what do you do in those "difficult" situations? What if you are caught in an embarrassing situation, don't we need to protect ourselves? What about the other guy? Truthtelling could make it embarrassing for him as well. Is it better to bend the truth a little, if necessary, in order to keep good community relations? Some persons say always tell the truth regardless. Others say that it depends on the situation. For instance, if some good can come out of speaking the untruth then the loving and positively right thing is to tell a lie. Do you argee? What is truthtelling? What is falsehood?

Is Truth Telling Always Right?

In the apostolic church era, believers often sold possessions, and gave money into a common treasury to be distributed according to the need. Ananias and Sapphira, a man and wife, sold a piece of property. The story goes that this couple brought their money to the apostles and left the impression that it was the entire amount received from the sale. God was displeased with such pretense, and Ananias and Sapphira died. No doubt this story raises some questions in your mind.

God Hates Pretense

What happened to Ananias and Sapphira is a speeded-up version of what happens to every man and woman who lives by falsehood. Some students made a science project by planting a seed next to a window and taking a picture every five minutes for several days. Then they made a movie of it. By bringing the beginning and the end together they

The Beginning and the End

made it look like it was happening all at once. In this story God brought the beginning and the end of falsehood together and we are shocked, for we are used to seeing the beginning of falsehood but not the end. Or we see the end but have forgotten about the beginning.*

Discuss
Think of illustrations of times a small untruth led to embarrassing and unhappy conclusions for you. Discuss the events which are set in motion by a lie.

"Mary isn't at home.
Would you like to leave
a rumor?"

Artist: Ivan Moon

*By Don Nofziger from **Herald Adult Bible Studies**

If falsehood had only to do with words and not with personhood then it might be considered a minor issue, but false words cannot be separated from the false person. This is why it is difficult to talk about telling a lie (with integrity, lovingly, making it positively right) so that some good may come about. Lies make people like puppets. They may act and look alive but are not for real. Falsehood is person-destroying. The irony is that most lies are told because persons want to protect or save themselves. The Christian can be honest because he had died to the old self that needs falsehood for protection.

Falsehood Destroys Personhood

Persecution from the outside enemies did not destroy the early church, so Satan strikes at the root and heart of the community life. He attacks at the point of truthtelling. If he can destroy trust then he has destroyed the new community. Community depends on communication. If the communication is false the community will fall apart. After trust is gone, whatever else may be left, is just empty form and lovelessness, not community. Paul says in Ephesians 4:25, "speak every man truth with his neighbour: for we are members one of another." Without trust real communication is impossible. By engaging in falsehoods you are not only hurting yourself, but injuring your circle of brothers. Genuine respect for my brother demands that you be truthful.

Falsehood Destroys Community

Read the paragraph "Is Truth Telling Always Right?" again. Is there a difference between protecting yourself by telling a falsehood and protecting the life of a brother by telling a falsehood? Discuss.

Discuss

57

1. Do the results you seek ever justify the means you use to achieve them? Check one below:

A. A big lie to protect someone. Yes———— No————
?————

B. Killing to save someone you love from being killed. Yes
————No———— ? ————

C. To be a Robin Hood, stealing, to feed the poor and needy.
Yes————No———— ? ————

2. Discuss times when you had to choose between one of two right things or courses of action.

3. Write to Internal Revenue, asking about fraud against the government by citizens. What statistics can you gather about the extent of preparing false tax returns in your state or province?

4. List some forms of dishonesty in the church, school, and society today. What is the remedy to dishonesty? How do we "speak the truth in love" by actions?

5. Why do people cheat? Who gains or loses from cheating? Are there degrees of cheating? Discuss.

6. Take time to share and discuss what persons have discovered from personal study and reflection in Phase One.

10. Does Money Really Satisfy?

By Lupe De Leon

Exodus 20:17

You shall not covet your neighbour's house; you shall not covet your neighbour's wife, his slave, his slave-girl, his ox, his ass, or anything that belongs to him.

Luke 12:15-21

Then he said to the people, "Beware! Be on your guard against greed of every kind, for even when a man has more than enough, his wealth does not give him life." And he told them this parable: "There was a rich man whose land yielded heavy crops. He debated with himself: 'What am I to do? I have not the space to store my produce. This is what I will do,' said he: 'I will pull down my store-houses and build them bigger. I will collect in them all my corn and other goods, and then say to myself, "Man, you have plenty of good things laid by, enough for many years: take life easy, eat, drink, and enjoy yourself."' But God said to him, 'You fool, this very night you must surrender your life; you have made your money — who will get it now?' That is how it is with the man who amasses wealth for himself and remains a pauper in the sight of God."

1 Timothy 6:6-10

And of course religion does yield high dividends, but only to the man whose resources are within him. We brought nothing into the world; for that matter we cannot take anything with us when we leave, but if we have food and covering we may rest content. Those who want to be rich fall into temptations and snares and many foolish harmful desires which plunge men into ruin and perdition. The love of money is the root of all evil things, and there are some who in reaching for it have wandered from the faith and spiked themselves on many thorny griefs.

1. The idea of being "rich toward God" or having "riches in heaven" is found in the following passages: Luke 18:22-30; Luke 12:13-21; Luke 12:32-40. Underline the phrases every time they occur. What attitude is required to "be rich toward" God?

What kinds of actions express the attitude? _____

Hearing God's Call

2. Read 1 Timothy 6:2b-11. I understand the central concept of the passage to be:
   a. not to use religion as a means to become rich
   b. all the material needs a person requires is to have enough food and clothing for survival
   c. rich have more temptations than poor
   d. desiring to be rich can lead to sorrow and unhappiness

3. Additional passages relevant to the topic are: Ecclesiastes 5:10 -- 6:2; 9:7-13; Proverbs 21:1-8.

Pray and Reflect

"O Father, teach me how to relate myself to this world in which I live and move. Teach me each day what it means to be generous. Teach me to live. Amen."

Doing God's Word

I want to become more generous by
   a. giving my time to
   b. listening to
   c. sharing my records with _____
   d. learning to know and care about
   e. _____
   f. _____

The more we have the more we want. Persons need to be able to discern between what they want and what they need. Material things have become an obsession with many people. Dad works himself silly by keeping two jobs and Mom works full time just to give the kids so-called necessities. The closets and dressers in our homes cannot hold all our "necessities." Is this fair to our parents and to us? Wouldn't it be nice to have Dad and Mom home with us part of the time?

Material Things Do Not Satisfy

Is a deluxe camper or a home on wheels necessary for a happy family vacation? How much "camping" experience can one really have while sleeping in an air-conditioned, shower-equipped home on wheels, plus the added distraction of a television set? As a rule, people don't go camping to watch TV; rather it is to enjoy God's marvelous nature. How can a "deluxe modern" camper enjoy the sounds of nature such as frogs and crickets close to a lake or river? What about the overwhelming sensation of seeing a deer before he sees you? Those of you who have experienced such a camping experience can share the thrill of these feelings.

An Example of Luxury

Artist: Joel Kauffmann

Keeping up, not with the Joneses, but with ourselves is the biggest hassle. A regular bicycle does not really satisfy us anymore. We acquire a 10-speed, minibike, and look forward to the first car and the snowmobile. Our clothes need to be "brand-named" and must follow the latest fashions. Will an overflowing wardrobe really satisfy us? Is the old cliche of "I don't have a thing to wear," ever heard in your group? The problem is not one of having fashionable things which we convince ourselves are "necessities."

Don't Blame the Joneses

A word to some of the more affluent persons who have tried to adopt a simpler life-style is in order. Faded jeans and patched jackets from Goodwill Industries are no assurance of being free from the tentacles of materialism. What about the $500 to $1,000 stereo sets at home, and in cars? What about the stack of expensive albums, 8-track tapes, and cassettes? In rebelling against the so-called evils of middle-class America, the outward expressions have not always been consistent with the inner life and values.

Don't Be Fooled

The news media inform us that "happy, cool, groovy, far out" rich people are taking their own lives: Janice Joplin, Jimi Hendrix, Jim Morrison, and Peter Duel were considered groovy, rich, and far out, and yet they took their own lives. Are you convinced that happiness and contentment are not necessarily brought about by money or riches? A young man at Goshen College gave up his shares in a company and gave all his money for the needs in Bangladesh. To be truly happy, persons must get next to the needs of specific situations. Needs are not necessarily catagorized as hunger, thirst, or other physical needs. But rather the most prevalent need is loneliness. We need to be sensitive to the needs of our peers.

The Sound of True Contentment?

One day as I was in a heavy session with a fellow brother, thinking out loud about my future, he asked me very seriously, "To which god are you going to sell your soul in order to achieve your goals? Will it be the entertainment world god, the political god, or some other god?" Sadly enough many people who obtain their material wealth have "crushed" somebody or some people on the way up the so-called ladder of success. Some have lost their families, some have sold their very souls.

Greed Kills

Artist:
Joel
Kauffmann

"EEK!! AN EMPTY HANGER!"

When children demand so much of their parents that parents need to work two jobs in order to supply the family with its "needs," the possibility of losing the family "love" is very real. A friend of mine would leave his family every year to work in the city to make more money to help his children measure up to their peers. As these years went by he became the annual Santa Claus but he was not a father coming home to his family. Eventually he and his wife and family were caught up in a turmoil of family separation. Are your demands contributing to a similar kind of pressure in your home?

A Family Destroyed

63

All Comes from God and Returns to God

All persons, young or old, will ultimately return to mother earth. The home and the neighborhood in which we live makes no difference on the day of judgment. One day all will need to give an account to God for their deeds. Instead of living by the philosophy, "Plant more corn to feed more hogs to buy more land to plant more corn to feed more hogs to buy more land," we need to remember that true wealth is a generous and compassionate life. This quality makes people rich in God's sight.

Some Searching Questions

"When all things have been said and done only what is done for Christ will last." All things ultimately will need to be accounted for. Do I covet more and more things to satisfy my ego? Have I confused "necessities" with "needs"? Am I becoming "rich toward God"? Think on these things.

PHASE 3

1. There are two classifications of things mentioned in this lesson: the things that we **want** and the things we **need**. Discuss the following questions:

A. How many pairs of shoes do I have?
B. How many dresses, shirts, slacks, etc., do I have?
C. How many of the above mentioned items do I really need?
D. These same "necessities" can be taken into the greater concern area such as family, home, church, state, and nation.

2. We are "things oriented" thanks to the expert advertising that floods our homes via TV, radio, and newspapers. In light of all the experts telling us what's "good" for us, how can we keep from being brainwashed by the advertising?

3. Discuss in your discovery group how members plan to be more generous.

11. The Great Commandment

By Henry Shank

Deuteronomy 6:4, 5

Hear, O Israel, the Lord is our God, one Lord, and you must love the Lord your God with all your heart and soul and strength.

Mark 12:28-34

Then one of the lawyers, who had been listening to these discussions and had noted how well he answered, came forward and asked him, "Which commandment is first of all?" Jesus answered, "The first is, 'Hear, O Israel: the Lord our God is the only Lord; love the Lord your God with all your heart, with all your soul, with all your mind, and with all your strength.' The second is this: 'Love your neighbour as yourself.' There is no other commandment greater than these." The lawyer said to him, "Well said, Master. You are right in saying that God is one and beside him there is no other. And to love him with all your heart, all your understanding, and all your strength, and to love your neighbour as yourself -- that is far more than any burnt offerings or sacrifices." When Jesus saw how sensibly he answered, he said to him, "You are not far from the kingdom of God."

Romans 13:8-10

Leave no claim outstanding against you, except that of mutual love. He who loves his neighbour has satisfied every claim of the law. For the commandments, "Thou shalt not commit adultery, thou shalt not kill, thou shalt not steal, thou shalt not covet," and any other commandment there may be, are all summed up in the one rule, "Love your neighbour as yourself." Love cannot wrong a neighbour; therefore the whole law is summed up in love.

1. Read Leviticus 19:15-18 and discover ways to love your neighbor like yourself.

**Hearing
God's
Word**

2. Read Deuteronomy 6:4, 5, a key passage in the Old Testament. The idea which captured my attention was (circle one):
   a. there is only one God
   b. God is personal
   c. loving God involves all of my being
   d. God's commandments are to be communicated from father to son in a variety of ways

3. Discover that the New Testament teaches that when a person loves he fulfills the intent of what the law was originally meant to do -- to create a faithful loving community. Matthew 5:17; Mark 12: 28-34; Romans 13:7-10.

H. Armstrong Roberts

Love is a daisy opening its petals to the sun.
Love is a daisy turning its smile to a child.
Know any faces with smiles all the way around?
Know any people who open themselves to God or to others more than a moment or so on Sunday? Or does this sound more familiar? Love is plucking daisy petals one by one, reciting -- "He loves me, he loves me not. . . ." If petal-plucking is more than play, it represents love as using others for the security one wants. Perhaps a daisy-shredder finds it hard to love because he hasn't turned his own face upward to receive enough of God's love to give away.

Night Blooming Cereus?*

A daisy opens to the sun, its energy source for life. Its petals stay fresh much as the Jesus-follower keeps his life uncluttered to receive God's love. God leaves us on earth to reflect His love to others, just as daisies are little suns to children and other friends. **A field of daisies brings the sun to earth!**

Face Up!

"Love," in English, means many things -- from admiring Julie's new outfit to "love is a giddy feeling." To lonely people love is a disappointment. **Agape love is opening oneself -- one's whole life and being -- to another person.**

Petals Out!

But let's notice how Jesus talks about love. His Bible, the Old Testament, gives us two summary statements which Jesus calls the key to eternal life. Luke 10:25. The seminary professor needed to do what he knew. We agree with the New Testament, however, that only the power God's Spirit brings can grow this kind of fruit in our lives. Moved by God's Spirit in His own life, Jesus did exactly what these commandments ask. That is filling the law full. God wants His people of all ages to love Him and to love each other. **The gospel is that Jesus fulfilled this law.**

Love Is Spirit-Fruit

*A cactus which blooms for only an hour at midnight.

Start with the Heart!

Life becomes truly eternal -- out of sight -- when one opens himself completely to God. Jesus was telling us about what He knew from His own human experience. Jesus talked nights with God, He rejoiced with Him at a wedding, He cried with Him about Lazarus, He struggled with Him in Gethsemane. (Whose will won?) God's love should open first our emotions to Him. **Sing, laugh, clap, cry; express to Him your doubt, fear, or anger; leap for joy when He does something new in your life.**

Eternal Minutes?

Jesus' life was completely open to His Father. (Soul means life in the Bible.) Jesus first gave all His days to God and then at the end of that Gethsemane struggle gave up His life. All my life? -- that would mean all my choices! Football, movies, money, clothes, Camaros, and how I spend my time -- if I've given God my life and He's made it eternal.

Power to Share

Jesus' strength got used up walking with God up and down those rocks, teaching, and healing. He did overtime when the crowd needed Him, and then spent nights recuperating by praying! Jesus said He left us here to carry on His work of loving, healing, teaching, suffering. We have strength to share when we accept the Spirit-power Jesus promised.

Get Your Head Straight

Jesus knew God from ages of creating and working with Him. We can get our heads straight on God only by seeing Him work -- in the Bible, in Jesus restoring a torn-up creation, in our own lives when we work along with Him.

The seminary professor's two spiritual laws were right on, Jesus said, but his head wasn't straight on what neighbor meant because he didn't start with his heart in his devotion.

Work with God long enough to get your theology straight, and you'll find He loves each person as much as any other. Mark tells us about a more sincere seminary professor who asked Jesus for the greatest commandment. But Jesus **wouldn't give the first without the second.** That is, I can't open my life to God without also opening my life to His children.

God-Love Includes Neighbor-Love

In the Luke account, Jesus tells the Samaritan story to illustrate who a neighbor is -- it's someone you meet somewhere, sometime. And if your time is God's time, then it belongs to the person who needs it most. **Jesus said the seminary professor would truly live if he let God have his time for anyone who needed it!**

Who Needs It Most?

Let's look where Jesus got His second command to see what it summarized. (See Leviticus 19:9-18.) God says we must treat the poor well, not bow to important people, refuse to slander anyone, and instead of carrying a grudge, talk it over with the other guy. These ideas are repeated in Matthew 18, Ephesians 4, and James 2, but God knew long ago that **we cannot keep on loving each other if we keep our anger inside, neither telling nor forgiving, just smoldering!**

Doing a Slow Burn?

In fact, holding grudges isn't even fair to ourselves; it clobbers joy and brings ulcers! Which leads to a final point: Jesus never said we should love others more than ourselves. He said we should be open to others -- their needs, their uniqueness, their gifts -- as much as we are to ourselves. Some of us find it hard to love others because we don't really love ourselves very much. God put us together to give and receive love at the same time. **Remember! You matter to God as much as anyone else does!**

God Loves You Also!

1. Write down a list (in order of importance) of the things you want most from life right now (not five years from now). Examples:
-- closer friendships
-- better grades
-- making the team
-- mag wheels
-- nicer wardrobe
-- acceptance of my ideas and talents

Think of someone else in your group who might want that same thing. Would your emotions, time, or money be available to help him achieve those goals as they are for yourself?

2. Some questions for reflection and discussion:
   A. Does your congregation look like a field of daisies?
   B. Do you personally major in heart, soul, mind, or strength-love?
   C. Which of these concerns is the strongest (and weakest) point of your denomination, congregation, and youth group?

3. An exercise for groups of three or four might help you to get started on this: Each person tells the group some of the things he wants most from life. Then each other member takes some concrete item on his person and offers it symbolically to the other to help achieve his goals. For example, someone might hand his wristwatch to another saying, "Gerry, this watch means I'm giving you one hour each week to study biology." Of course, the objects can be returned following the time of sharing.

4. Discuss your responses to Phase One.

12. The Undisciplined Person

By Mark Yantzi

Proverbs 23:19-21, 29-35

Listen, my son, listen, and become wise;
set your mind on the right course.
Do not keep company with drunkards
or those who are greedy for the fleshpots;
for drink and greed will end in poverty,
and drunken stupor goes in rags....
Whose is the misery? whose the remorse?
Whose are the quarrels and the anxiety?
Who gets the bruises without knowing why?
Whose eyes are bloodshot?
Those who linger late over their wine,
those who are always trying some new spiced liquor.
Do not gulp down the wine, the strong red wine,
when the droplets form on the side of the cup;
in the end it will bite like a snake
and sting like a cobra.
Then your eyes see strange sights;
your wits and your speech are confused;
you become like a man tossing out at sea,
like one who clings to the top of the rigging;
you say, "If it lays me flat, what do I care?
If it brings me to the ground, what of it?
As soon as I wake up,
I shall turn to it again."

1 Corinthians 10:12, 13

If you feel sure that you are standing firm, beware! You may fall. So far you have faced no trial beyond what man can bear. God keeps faith, and he will not allow you to be tested above your powers, but when the test comes he will at the same time provide a way out, by enabling you to sustain it.

1. Read Galatians 5:13-24 and discover two contrasting life-styles.

Life of Love in the Spirit

An Undisciplined Life

Hearing God's Word

2. Read Matthew 5:13-16 and put your name in place of the pronoun "you." Read it again and put the name of your congregation in place of the pronoun "you." Which are the most important ways to be salt and light?

   -- individual purity
   -- radical life-style of love
   -- involvement in the needs of society
   -- separation from society

3. I have difficulty disciplining my life in the following areas:

_____

_____

_____

_____

Mind on Right Course

It is quite easy to picture a father speaking to his teenage son in Proverbs 23:19-21. His one hand on the son's shoulder and the other pointing a direction, he tells the son to set his mind on the "right course." And that's really where the whole discipline thing begins. It's not refraining from certain activities and doing others, but rather in having a mind which is on the right course. Then do's and don'ts won't be a problem.

Some time ago I had a toothache. Without hesitation I reached for the aspirin bottle, because I do not enjoy pain. Modern medicine makes it possible to alleviate pain and provide for greater personal comfort which is fine. But with my toothache, I knew why the tooth was aching -- it was because I had earlier neglected to properly care for my teeth. Later when the results of my lack of discipline became "painfully" clear, I wanted to avoid the consequences. After reflecting on the situation briefly, I compromised and took two aspirins rather than three.
-- Should I have taken any aspirins?
-- Is there any merit in suffering for past failures?

A Toothache

In recent years there has been a great deal of publicity concerning the use of illegal drugs, somewhat overshadowing the use of alcohol, a legal drug. The LeDain Commission on the nonmedical use of drugs in Canada stated that "dependence on alcohol is a problem 100 times more serious than dependence on other drugs." In France, the heaviest drinking country in the world, patients with alcohol-related diseases now occupy 50 percent of all hospital beds. This is not to minimize the effects of illegal drugs. There are harmful effects, and aside from physical effects there are legal and criminal sanctions. The warning given by the writer of Proverbs to the son concerning the impovershing effects of alcohol was not without foundation.

Drugs End in Poverty

Today the alcoholic or "alkie" has become a symbol of despair. Often he is seen in drama or films to provide humor. We laugh at his swaying steps and slurred speech. The writer of Proverbs had obviously witnessed this. His description of confused wits and speech and the seeing of strange sights is quite pointed. The symptoms of intoxication have changed

A Different World

little, but the world sure has! In a machine age the consequences of the excessive use of alcohol or drugs are greatly magnified. When a person under the influence of a drug including alcohol drives a car or performs other tasks requiring precision, the lives of many people are endangered.

Sick or Irresponsible?

Alcohol dependency can be dealt with as a criminal matter or it can be looked on as a disease. The alcoholic is definitely sick, but his disease is not alcoholism. It is his own shirking of responsibility and discipline. Drug use is often an escape as well. No one wants to become an alcoholic because alcoholism implies an inability to control drinking. The only sure way to avoid the problem is not to drink at all. This has been a common Christian stance. Recently, however, social drinking has become more accepted in some circles.

-- How relevant is a discussion of alcoholism to you?

-- Do I have "alcoholic symptoms," i.e., shirking of responsibility and discipline?

-- What are the pros and cons of social drinking?

Tons of Excess

A lack of discipline can be seen in various areas. The Proverbs passage indicates several. Gluttonous eating habits, implied in "greedy for the fleshpots" may strike close home. North Americans daily carry with them, tons of excess weight, which is not without its consequences. It is a prime cause of heart attacks. Eventually it "stings."

-- Am I able to discipline myself against overeating?

Inner and Outer Discipline

"Discipline" isn't a popular word these days. "Doing your own thing" implies the opposite; a freedom from restrictions. It seems there are two types of discipline. There's inner discipline which regulates action from within the person, and external discipline which is brought to bear on the individual from parents, teachers, and acquaintances. The strength of self-discipline can best be seen when there are no restraining forces from outside.

-- Are you controlled by your environment or from within?

-- How is self-discipline developed?

Going Deeper

To talk about discipline without mentioning what lies behind it would make the discussion shallow and incomplete. Whether discipline is applied to one's personal life, to relationships with parents, or a school classroom, the principle is the same. Without a deeper motivation which goes beyond outer controls, discipline becomes a sham. A student who for some reason does not want to be taught, can be restrained by external forces, but cannot be disciplined to change his attitude toward schoolwork. **If the rigorous demands of Jesus for His disciples are maintained today, it is because the discipline or discipleship springs from an inner commitment to the way of Jesus.**

PHASE 3

1. Discuss in your discovery group the areas in which you find it difficult to discipline your life.

2. This week I plan to take the following steps to concretely improve my self-discipline:

SIGNED--------------------------------------

_____

_____

_____

_____

3. Draw a cartoon with simple line drawings. Use the caption:

DISCIPLINE IS. . . .

13. How Can I Help?

By Mark Yantzi

Mark 2:16, 17

Some doctors of the law who were Pharisees noticed him eating in this bad company, and said to his disciples, "He eats with tax-gatherers and sinners!" Jesus heard it and said to them, "It is not the healthy that need a doctor, but the sick; I did not come to invite virtuous people, but sinners."

Galatians 5:25 –– 6:5

If the Spirit is the source of our life, let the Spirit also direct our course.

We must not be conceited, challenging one another to rivalry, jealous of one another. If a man should do something wrong, my brothers, on a sudden impulse, you who are endowed with the Spirit must set him right again very gently. Look to yourself, each one of you: you may be tempted too. Help one another to carry these heavy loads, and in this way you will fulfill the law of Christ.

For if a man imagines himself to be somebody, when he is nothing, he is deluding himself. Each man should examine his own conduct for himself; then he can measure his achievement by comparing himself with himself and not with anyone else. For everyone has his own proper burden to bear.

PHASE 1

Read Galatians 5:25 –– 6:5 and Mark 2:16, 17 several times and paraphrase it in your own words. Additional passages to study: Luke 15:11-32; 1 Corinthians 9:19-23.

What are some "burdens" you bear? How can others help you?

Young people sometimes have the opportunity to attend special regional or denominational youth conventions. Exposed to committed speakers and creative leadership, many youth return home with a renewed Christian commitment and full of enthusiasm to share this joy with others. Faced again with the home situation, the question is sure to arise, "How can I help?"

How can the ideals and hopes of this mountaintop experience be converted into productive action?

It may be helpful to look at a number of steps in making the jump from the mountaintop to the home experience:

Getting into Action

There must be a belief that God can change people and situations dramatically. Last week's lesson dealt with undisciplined persons. This week we look to the example of Jesus in dealing with "bad characters." Supporting one another, and in that way helping each other carry the sometimes heavy load, is of prime importance.

Step One

Persons wishing to help must have an awareness of what the problem is. Can you imagine going to help a poor family without having discussed their need of help or whether, in fact, your help is wanted? It is very important to have the facts straight before getting involved.

Step Two

The proper attitude toward the person or persons to whom you are relating is most important. Too often a "holier than thou" attitude is projected. Talking isn't always the most effective way to convey love. Sometimes we had best "stifle" and let thoughtful acts or just plain listening, show our concern.

Step Three

Prejudiced Youth?

A number of years ago, an acquaintance from a drop-in center came along to church. He was a member of the "Third Reich" motorcycle club and wore high boots, jeans, and a studded leather jacket. The reaction was interesting. The adults, somewhat surprised, seemingly accepted him, at least they spoke to him and welcomed him. To the youth, however, he was apparently a bad character. Throughout the church service and Sunday school, there were sly glances at his outlandish clothes and whispers and snickers. No youth came to talk. — It's easy to write off adults as "old fogies" who are prejudiced, but what about youth?

An Uncle Tom

Levi was certainly a person who needed help. He was an "Uncle Tom" who had finked out and gone to collect taxes for the hated Romans. That meant no respectable Jew would associate with him and he therefore associated with other outcast "bad characters." Jesus saw beyond the prejudiced opinions of the people around Him. No doubt many of the claims of excessive collection of taxes were justified. Yet Jesus was prepared to hang around with Levi despite criticism from the enraged Pharisees. But we don't have to go it alone. Faced with personal frustrations and persons in need of love there is a need for others to help. "Everyone has his own proper burden to bear," but we don't have to each go it alone. Some would say, "Put up a bold front and show to the world that you are coping." The way of Jesus, however, is to "help one another carry these heavy loads." That implies admitting when things really get us down and also helping someone else who is having a hard time. That is what is meant by "brotherhood." Sometimes in our large congregations it becomes difficult to practice brotherhood in a meaningful way.

Bill is living in Yourtown now but has lived in a lot of other towns before. In fact he has never spent one full year at one school. Because of his family's frequent moving he has attended as many as three schools in one year. He hates school and the teachers are always on his back. At home there's always chaos. Bill is the oldest of eight children, and shares a room with his three brothers. His father, who because of a serious operation is unable to work, is usually drunk or drinking and always shouting. For Bill home is as distasteful as school. When Dad shouts and Mom whines and his brothers and sisters are quarreling, he walks out slamming the door to the small, shabby, rundown house. It is only two blocks to the pool hall. That is where he meets his friends and feels, at least a bit, that he belongs.

The Story of Bill (A Case Study)

Tonight as he enters the pool hall, everything is hushed. Then he notices two tall men wearing a suit and tie. Obviously cops. They want to talk to Bill about a house break-in. A person was seen running from the house. He looked like Bill. He refuses to talk and is taken to the police station for questioning, which lasts for several hours. Finally, he is put in a cell for the remainder of the night. At home his three brothers have a bit more room. They don't mind his absence. The next morning he appears before a judge. He could have spoken to a legal aid lawyer but declined. The question is asked, "How do you plead to this charge, guilty or not guilty?" There is a pause, then Bill shrugs his shoulder and replies, "Guilty." The court is told briefly of Bill's home background, and while the judge scolds Bill for his apparent misbehavior, he is also quite sympathetic. Bill does not want sympathy. He is placed on probation for one year and goes directly from court to the probation office and waits.

PHASE 3

1. Yourtown has a volunteer probation program whereby persons on probation are supervised by community persons. With one person taking the part of Bill and another that of the volunteer, do a role play from the point where Bill is waiting. Other persons who wish to may step behind either Bill or the volunteer and gives replies or ask questions.

2. Check back to the three steps mentioned earlier in this lesson. Do they apply to this situation? Did Bill commit the crime of which he was convicted? Share about persons in your experience who remind you of Bill.

3. This week you may wish to investigate what possibilities are available in your community for volunteers.

4. Close with prayer to support each other in the heavy loads you have to carry.

Postscript

1. The high point in this study "Discover Life" was _____

_____

_____

2. The greatest thing about life I have discovered is _____

_____

3. The areas where I need further understanding and help are

_____

_____

For further group study of Christian life-style consider **Rap** by Lyman Coleman, available from Serendipity House, Scottdale, PA 15683. This is an excellent study including relational labs, spiritual encounters, and enabling sessions.